HELP!
Tooth Fairy is in Trouble

By Effin Older

Bunny Farm Press
Chickamauga, GA USA

HELP! TOOTH FAIRY IS IN TROUBLE By Effin Older
Published by Bunny Farm Press, an imprint of Three Ravens
Publishing
threeravenspublishing@gmail.com
P O Box 851, Chickamauga, Ga 30707
https://www.threeravenspublishing.com
Copyright © 2025 by Effin Older

Credits:
HELP! TOOTH FAIRY IS IN TROUBLE was written by Effin
Older

HELP! TOOTH FAIRY IS IN TROUBLE by: Effin Older /Bunny
Farm Press-Three Ravens Publishing – 1st edition, 2025

Ebook ISBN: 978-1-966507-39-0
Trade Paperback ISBN: 978-1-966507-40-6
Hardback ISBN: 978-1-966507-41-3

Dedication

This is dedicated to

Jules

and

Willow and Amber

Best. Editors. Ever!

Table of Contents

Chapter 1.. 1

Chapter 2.. 9

Chapter 3.. 15

Chapter 4.. 19

Chapter 5.. 23

Chapter 6.. 29

Chapter 7.. 33

Chapter 8.. 39

Chapter 9.. 47

Chapter 10 53

Chapter 11 57

Chapter 12 59

Chapter 13 63

Chapter 14 67

Chapter 15 71

Chapter 16 75

Chapter 17 79

Chapter 18 85

Chapter 19 91

Chapter 20 95

Chapter 21 99

Chapter 22 103

Chapter 1

In a little cottage in Lilac Village, the Twinkles were eating their favorite dinner — spaghetti and meatballs.

"Delicious," said Mr. Twinkle. He pushed his chair back from the table and stood up. "Anybody else want seconds?"

"Me," said four-year-old Washington, rubbing his tummy. "Yum in tum."

Mrs. Twinkle shook her head. "Not for me. I'm leaving room for dessert."

Tulip stabbed her last meatball with a fork. "I've got one more bite," she said, popping the whole meatball into her mouth and starting to chew.

One chew.

Two chews.

Three chews.

Suddenly, Tulip stopped chewing. Her eyes grew big. She touched her lower lip with her fingers. "Uh-oh," she said quietly, "I think … I think

I've — "

"You've what?" her mother interrupted. "Is something the matter?"

"I think I've lost my tooth!"

"Goodness!" Mrs Twinkle exclaimed. "Let me see!"

With her mouth full of meatball, Tulip bared her teeth in a big, fake smile and pulled down her lower lip. Right where there should be a tooth, there was no tooth. There was a gap.

Washington eyeballed the gap. "Where toof?" he asked.

Mr. Twinkle also eyeballed the gap. "Did you swallow it?"

"I don't think so," Tulip answered through clenched teeth. She leaned over her plate and spat out the meatball. She poked it. She pushed it. She bent down close to examine it. "It's not here."

Washington leaned over and bent down even closer to Tulip's plate. "Toof not in meeball. Toof gone."

"I'm sure I didn't swallow it." Tulip cut the meatball into tiny little pieces. It felt all mushy and squishy and not one bit toothy. "What if I can't find it?" She was close to tears. "It's the first tooth I've ever lost!"

"Look again," suggested her father. "If you didn't swallow, it's got to be there."

Tulip cut the meatball into even smaller bits. Just as she was about to burst into real tears, she felt something. Something not mushy and squishy. Something? … maybe? … *toothy*? She put down the knife and shmooshed the meatball with her fingers. And there it was — a little, pure-white baby tooth, dotted with bits of meatball.

All four Twinkles studied the tooth as if they'd never seen anything like it. "The Tooth Fairy will be delighted to get such a perfect tooth," said Mrs. Twinkle. "You should tell her right away."

"Tooth Fairy?" Tulip rolled her eyes. "Mom, I'm seven-going-on-eight, remember? I don't think I'll write — "

"You don't think you'll write to the Tooth Fairy?"

"That's not *exactly* what I mean, Mom. I'm just not sure

she — "

"Me wite Toof Faiwy," Washington interrupted. "Give Toof Faiwy shiny shells."

Tulip rolled her eyes again. "Oh, Washington, the Tooth Fairy doesn't collect shiny shells. She collects teeth."

Mrs. Twinkle ruffled Washington's hair. "Don't worry. She'll want *your* teeth, too, when the time comes." Mrs. Twinkle turned to Tulip. "Want me to look through my notecards and pick a pretty one for your letter to her? Fairies like pretty things."

Tulip shrugged. "I suppose. And I'd better brush my tooth so it's nice and shiny. Want a shmooshed meatball, Truffle?"

At the sound of his name, the floppy-eared basset hound trotted over to his dish and quickly licked up what was left of the meatball.

By the time Tulip had brushed the meatball from her tooth and found her colored pens, Mrs. Twinkle had chosen a flowery note card and a matching envelope. "Have you thought about what you're going to write?"

Tulip nodded, picked a purple pen, and wrote:

Dear Tooth Fairy,

I lost my first tooth today. I almost swallowed it

when it got stuck in a meatball. My mom says you would

love to have it, so here it is, all brushed and shiny.

I wonder what you'll do with it. I guess I'll never know.

This may be my last letter to you.

Love, Tulip

PS. I have a book about Fairies. I hope it's all true.

Mrs. Twinkle smiled. "That's a beautiful letter. I'm sure the Tooth Fairy will be very pleased. Now, it's nearly bedtime, so hop into your PJs. You want to be sound asleep for the Tooth Fairy."

"You mean, like for Santa? I have to be asleep or she won't come?"

Mrs. Twinkle smiled. "Something like that. And that goes for you, too, Washington. The Tooth Fairy doesn't want to be caught collecting teeth. Don't ask me why. That's just the way it is and ..." she paused, "and always will be."

Tulip tucked her letter into the envelope, dropped in her tooth, licked the seal, and slid the envelope under her pillow. The last thing she did before drifting off to sleep was to slide the tip of her tongue into the new gap between her teeth.

Chapter 2

The next thing Tulip heard was a soft, fluttery, humming sound. Still half asleep, she flicked at her ear like she was flicking away a mosquito. The humming didn't stop. She flicked again and turned over. More humming. "Go away!" Tulip yelped, sitting up straight in bed. "Go away!"

Tulip's yelp woke her brother. "Toof Faiwy come?" he asked, rubbing his eyes. "Take toof?"

Tulip felt under her pillow. "Nope, it's still here. We'd better go back to sleep or she won't come. Mom said!"

"Me sweep," mumbled Washington, settling down in his bed.

"Me, too." Tulip rolled over, closed her eyes, and said to herself, *I bet she won't come, but I'll pretend anyway … for Washington's sake.*

Seconds after Tulip pulled the blanket back up to her chin and closed her eyes, the soft, fluttery humming began again. This time, she didn't bother to flick it away. She switched on her unicorn nightlight to get a better look. At first, she couldn't see anything unusual. Then, she thought maybe … maybe she *might* see something. Something hazy floating above her bed.

She rubbed her eyes. She blinked three times. She rubbed her eyes again and looked up toward the ceiling. *Am I dreaming?* She sat up straighter in bed. "Looks sorta' like a fairy," she mumbled, loud enough to wake Washington again.

"Faiwy come? Where?"

Tulip pointed up.

Washington looked up. "Toof Faiwy?"

"Maybe. I'll see if it talks." Tulip cleared her throat. "Ahem. Excuse me, but are you the Tooth Fairy?"

"Shhhh, don't wake your parents," came a soft reply.

"Whoa! It talks!"

"Of course," the fairy said in a honey-soft voice. "What did you expect?"

"I ... I ... didn't expect ... I mean, I wasn't sure about — "

"About fairies? Yes, I *am* a fairy and, no, you're not dreaming." The fairy had now silently drifted down and settled at the foot of Tulip's bed. "I'm not *the* Tooth Fairy. That's Queen Quinella. I'm Poppy."

Washington's eyes popped wide open. "Whoa! Faiwy come!"

At the sound of the word *come*, Truffle hopped off his cozy, donut-shaped bed and jumped onto Washington's bed. The little box hitched to Truffle's collar rattled. Inside were bone-shaped doggie treats. The treats were supposed to *persuade* Truffle to obey a command.

Tulip ignored Truffle and studied the fairy from the tip of her bare feet to the tiara twinkling on her head. She was a little taller than Washington. In her hand was a silver-tipped wand. She wore a lacy, cherry-red dress and a necklace of sparkly, heart-shaped rubies. Her wings shimmered in shades of scarlet, garnet, and candy-apple red.

She does look a lot like the fairies in my book, Tulip admitted to herself.

Once Tulip decided she wasn't dreaming and there really *was* a fairy sitting on her bed, she asked, "I don't mean to be rude, but why are you here? I mean, uh … I lost my first tooth, and I wrote to the Tooth Fairy, but — "

"I know," Poppy interrupted.

"You know? How did you know?"

Washington burst in. "Tooyip toof in meeball!"

Poppy smiled. "I know about that, too, but right now, I have something more important on my mind. I'm here because of Queen Quinella. She's in trouble and needs *your* help."

"Wait! Who *is* Queen Quinella?"

"She's the Tooth Fairy queen. I'm one of the fairies in her court."

"So, let me get this straight. You're *not* the queen, but you're a *real* fairy?"

Poppy nodded. "I'm as real as they get." She held up one hand. "Please, please, no more questions. You'll understand everything once we get to Shimmer-Shire."

"I've never heard of Shimmer-Shire."

"It's Queen Quinella's queendom. It's where I live, and

where — "

Tulip sat upright in bed. She looked Poppy straight in the eye. "I'm really sorry about Queen Quinella and her troubles … whatever they are … but I think you've made a big mistake. I'm seven-going-on-eight, and I only wrote to the Tooth Fairy because Mom said —"

Poppy interrupted. "I know all that, too, but Queen Quinella *needs* you. I don't have time to explain. It'll become clear soon enough. Pleeezze, will you come?"

Tulip took a deep breath and let it out slowly. "This is all too, too weird but, okay, I'll come ... under one condition."

Poppy smiled for the first time. "Name it."

"I'll come only if Washington comes, too ... and Truffle. I don't go anywhere without them."

"Done!"

"Well, that was easy," Tulip mumbled.

Poppy and Tulip bumped fists to close the deal.

Truffle woofed. Washington hopped out of bed. "Me see Toof Faiwy! Me see Toof Faiwy!"

"Please hurry," Poppy begged. "I'll wait for you outside."

And like a puff of cloud, the fairy disappeared.

Chapter 3

Tulip threw off the blanket and hopped out of bed. Still in their PJs, Tulip and Washington tiptoed outside. Truffle padded silently behind. Tulip spotted Poppy's twinkling tiara right away. The fairy was perched on top of the front gate ... waiting.

"We're ready," Tulip said. "This better be a good idea." She looked around. "So, where's your car?"

Poppy burst out laughing. "Car? Have you ever heard of a fairy riding in a car? Or a truck? Or on an electric scooter?"

"Uh ... no," Tulip said, a little embarrassed. "But I've also never seen a fairy sitting on my front gate."

"Fair enough," Poppy agreed. "I'll give you 10 seconds to figure out how I'll get you to Shimmer-Shire."

One second, two seconds ... nine seconds, 10 seconds. No answer from Tulip.

"Here's a hint," the fairy said. With a soft, fluttery humming of her wings, Poppy slowly drifted up, up, up off the gate.

"What!" Tulip exclaimed. "Are you kidding me? We're *flying?*"

Poppy didn't bother to answer. She drifted back down and hovered over the three Twinkles. With her wand, she gently brushed fairy dust on the head of each Twinkle. In an instant, pink, butterfly-shaped wings appeared on their backs. In another instant, the three Twinkles were drifting slowly up, up, and up. They drifted up over the fence around their house, up over the bedroom where their parents lay sleeping, and up over all the other cottages in Lilac Village.

"Me frying!" Washington exclaimed.

"Me frying, too!" echoed Tulip.

Truffle woofed and paddled his short legs like he was swimming.

"Follow me," Poppy called. "We'll be in Shimmer-Shire in no time. When we get there, you'll learn why Queen Quinella needs you."

Chapter 4

Powered by their soft, fluttery wings, the three Twinkles gazed in amazement as they floated past Lilac Village, and over flower-covered meadows, and babbling brooks, and forests of leafy green trees. Tulip even spotted a deer resting on a bed of colorful leaves. She pinched herself several times to be sure she wasn't dreaming.

"We're almost to Shimmer-Shire," Poppy called. "It's just beyond that hillock over there."

Tulip looked to where Poppy pointed. "What's a hillock?"

"A hillock is what we fairies call a small hill. All the other hillocks around here have flat or pointy tops. For some strange reason, that's the only one with a round dome top. And it has those wonky-looking tree-thingies sticking out of it."

Tulip glanced at the hillock as she glided past. She didn't have time to look closely, but something about that round dome looked familiar. It gave her tummy flutters. *But, how could it be familiar?* she asked herself. *I've never been here before ... and yet ...* She wished she could spend more time checking it out, but Poppy was getting too far ahead. Afraid she'd lose sight of the fairy, Tulip pushed her curiosity about the dome to the back of her mind.

Tulip forgot about the strange hillock the instant she spotted where Poppy, Washington, and Truffle had landed. They were standing beside a sign with big, glowing letters along the top. The letters spelled the word **SHIMMER-SHIRE**. Colored lights and blossoms in shades of pink, purple, and plum outlined the sign. Under the word **SHIMMER-SHIRE** it said,

LAND OF ENCHANTMENT

Tulip drifted silently down and alighted next to Poppy. For a moment, just for a moment, she was speechless. Then, her eyes popped wide open.

"Look!" She pointed to a bright rainbow behind a giant castle on a hill.

"Look!" She pointed to fairies flying around little red-and-white cottages with window boxes filled with yellow daisies.

"Look!" She pointed to flower gardens, and leafy green trees, and ponds full of lily pads.

"Look!" She pointed to real, live unicorns that reminded her of her own unicorn lamp.

Poppy tapped Tulip on the shoulder. "There'll be plenty of time later to check out everything but, right now, we need to see Queen Quinella."

Tulip was so fascinated with what she saw, she'd forgotten about why Poppy needed her. Then, she remembered. "But … but what if Washington and Truffle and I can't help and — " Tulip began.

"Please. No ifs, ands, or buts. I have every confidence Queen Quinella made the best choice when she chose you. She never makes mistakes when it comes to kids. Now, c'mon, we can't keep her waiting any longer."

Once again, Poppy tapped the three Twinkles on their heads with her wand and, the next thing they knew, their feet left the ground. The soft, fluttery humming of wings was the only sound they heard as they flew over Shimmer-Shire to the castle of the Queen of Tooth Fairies.

Chapter 5

As the shimmering castle came closer into view, Tulip thought she'd never seen anything so beautiful. It had five towers — one tall one and four shorter ones. A flag fluttered from the top of each tower. Each flag was a different color. A moat filled with darting orange fish and beds of white lily pads surrounded the castle. Arching over the moat were five yellow-and-white-striped bridges leading to each of the towers. One bridge ended at a golden front door that led into the tallest tower. Now, as she stood in front of that door with Poppy, Washington, and Truffle, Tulip noticed the most amazing thing of all — the castle was made entirely of teeth!

There were hundreds … no thousands, millions, gazillions, bajillions — (Tulip made up *bajillions* because she didn't know what comes after gazillions) — of shiny, white, baby teeth just like the one she almost lost in the meatball. *So, that's where they go*, Tulip said to herself. *The castle is huge; no wonder Queen Quinella needs so many teeth.*

Poppy knocked lightly on the golden front door.

She waited.

She knocked again.

This time, the door opened, just a crack; then it opened wider. "I've brought Tulip and — " Poppy began.

A fairy who looked like a shorter version of Poppy stepped outside. "Shhhh," she said, touching her finger to her lips. "Queen Quinella is napping. Come back in a little while, okay?"

Poppy nodded and said to the Twinkles, "This is Pansy, my little sister. Queen Quinella is our big sister. We live in this tower."

Tulip finger-waved to Pansy and whispered, "Hi."

Pansy waved back, then whispered to Poppy, "How about telling our guests all about the castle while you're waiting. It won't be long."

"Great idea. See you soon."

Pansy slipped back into the tower and gently closed the door.

"Follow me," Poppy said as she rose slightly above the bridge and glided back across the moat, followed by three gliding Twinkles.

When everyone was across and their feet were again on the ground, Poppy turned and pointed back to the castle. "Queen Quinella and Pansy and I live in the tallest tower, the one with the silver flag. No one ever enters that tower without a special invitation."

"Why?" Tulip wondered.

Poppy cleared her throat. "Besides being where our Queen lives, it has two other very special things."

"Like what?"

"Well, one is the QQ-Ding."

Tulip scrunched up her nose. "I've never heard of a QQ-Ding."

"QQ stands for Queen Quinella … obviously … and a 'ding' is the sound my sister hears when someone loses a tooth. No one else hears it; not even me or Pansy."

"That's clever," Tulip said. "What's the other special thing?"

"Her QQ-Globe. What do you think that might be for?"

Tulip scrunched up her nose again. "Hmmmm." She thought for a minute. "QQ stands for Queen Quinella — "

Poppy nodded. "Right so far."

"And … and … I know!" Tulip grinned. "A globe is a round map of the world, so — "

"And this globe lights up!" Poppy quickly added.

Suddenly, Tulip clapped her hands and jumped up and down. "So, when Queen Quinella hears a 'ding,' the globe lights up to show her where to collect the baby tooth. Am I right?"

"Right again and …" Poppy paused and now looked very serious. "And if Queen Quinella didn't have the QQ-Ding and the QQ-Globe, someone *pretending* to be the real Tooth Fairy might try to steal the children's precious teeth."

Tulip stamped her foot. "That would be awful! Queen Quinella wouldn't get the children's letters, and *they* wouldn't get her special gift. That must not happen!"

Chapter 6

Poppy nodded. "Exactly. Now, while the Queen naps, I'll tell you about the other towers. See the tower with the red flag? That's where Catcher and Cricket, the tooth keepers, live."

"Toof keepa?" Washington asked.

"They guard the teeth. They also crush them into sparkling, magical fairy dust, just like the dust from my wand that I sprinkled on you so you could — "

"Fry!" Washington burst out. "Duss make me fry!"

Poppy smiled. "Exactly." She pointed to another tower. "See the blue tower? That's Fairy Feast. It's the café where Figaro and Fantasia make all the things fairies love to eat — fresh fruit smoothies and honey cookies and fairy cakes and — "

"Fruit smoothies are my favorite," Tulip interrupted.

"Me yike honey cookie," Washington added, smacking his lips.

"I'm sure you'll get to try both," Poppy said, "but right now we'd better get back to the Queen."

On the way, Tulip asked about the tower with the green flag.

"That's Miraculous Magic. It's where fairies learn all about the art of making … " Poppy paused. "Anyone? Anyone?"

Washington's hand shot up. "Magic!"

Poppy smiled and nodded. "Clever boy. Marlin and Maxima are the best magic makers ever."

Tulip pointed to the last tower with the yellow flag. "What's special about that tower?"

"That's Awesome Amusements. Inside is a huge dragon-shaped bouncy castle. There are also slides and swings and climbing walls and tunnels and bumper cars and …" Poppy stopped naming all the other kinds of awesome amusements because, by this time, they were now back at Queen Quinella's golden front door.

And Tulip was about to find out why the Tooth Fairy Queen was in such terrible trouble.

Chapter 7

Poppy tapped lightly on the door. Almost immediately, it swung open. There stood Pansy, motioning for Poppy and the Twinkles to come inside. "I was about to come looking for you. QQ has awakened and is eager to meet our very special guests." (QQ was what Poppy and Pansy called their big sister, even though she was ever-so royal.) Pansy turned to Tulip and Washington. "You may call her QQ, too. I have to admit that Queen Quinella is quite a mouthful."

Tulip agreed, but she was too polite to say so.

"How's our sister?" Poppy asked.

"Rested and ready."

Ready for what? Tulip wondered. She hoped it would be something like showing her inside the other four towers, especially Fairy Feast. The excitement of losing her first baby tooth, meeting a real, live fairy, and flying to Shimmer-Shire had left her starving. "If you ask me, a quick stop at Fairy Feast for a fresh fruit smoothie would hit the spot," Tulip suggested.

Pansy ignored her suggestion. "Please follow me to QQ's private chamber. The sooner you come up with a plan for her troubles, the better. Time is running out."

Tulip looked puzzled. "A plan? I ... I don't have a plan." All of a sudden, she felt not just puzzled and hungry; she felt worried. Yes, it was all fun and games meeting Poppy, and flying, and seeing the fairy castle. But getting the Tooth Fairy Queen out of some kind of trouble? That was another thing altogether. A *scary* other thing. "Wait a minute!" Tulip burst out. "I *do* have a plan! A perfect plan! How about if QQ asks a *different* kid to come up with a plan?"

Again, Pansy ignored her suggestion.

Poppy gently squeezed Tulip's shoulder. "Remember, I told you Queen Quinella never, ever makes mistakes when it comes to kids. She can tell the brave from the fearful and the brainy from the brainless."

"Really? Does she think I'm — "

Poppy nodded. "She doesn't just *think* it. She *knows* it. Without a doubt, you're brave *and* brainy."

For a moment, Tulip thought *Maybe I am brave and brainy,* but that thought disappeared in a flash. She felt just the opposite … and also extremely worried. No matter what QQ's problem was, how could she, Tulip, just seven-going-on-eight, come up with a brave and brainy plan for the Queen of Tooth Fairies?

But there was no turning back now. With hunger rumbling in her tummy, Tulip, together with Washington and Truffle, followed the two fairy sisters to the very exclusive, very private chamber of Queen Quinella.

Pansy tapped three times on the chamber door.

"Do come in," said a sweet voice.

Pansy opened the door and stepped aside so the Twinkles could enter the royal room.

At first sight, "Yikes! Double yikes!" was all Tulip could say. There, in front of her very own eyes, sat Queen Quinella, the real, live, actual Tooth Fairy! She was sitting on a throne made of gold and decorated with little golden unicorns. On her head rested a five-pointed silver crown. Her filmy white dress sparkled with glitter. In her hand, she held a golden wand with a glittering, five-pointed star on the end.

Once Tulip could say something besides "Yikes!" she whispered to Poppy, "Should I kneel? I've never met a fairy queen before ..." she paused, "... actually, I've never met any kind of queen before, so I'm not sure what — "

Queen Quinella heard her question. "There's no need for kneeling. I'm just so happy to see you." She paused for a moment. "And you, too, Washington, and that darling puppy."

"Twuffle *dog*, not puppy," Washington quickly put in.

Tulip poked Washington. "Shhh, don't correct the Queen," she whispered without moving her lips.

Queen Quinella smiled. "You're right, Washington. How silly of me. Anyway, thank you, Twinkles, for coming. Now let me tell you why I need your help. I'm afraid I'm in big, big trouble here at Shimmer-Shire."

Chapter 8

Queen Quinella waved her wand and three red, velvet cushions suddenly appeared on the floor next to her delicate feet. The Queen motioned for the Twinkles to sit on the pillows, then cleared her throat. "For ever and ever, we fairies have lived at Shimmer-Shire in peace and harmony. I've collected baby teeth from all over the world and used them to build beautiful things like this castle and — "

"It's the most beautiful castle ever," Tulip murmured. She immediately felt a pat on her shoulder and turned to see Poppy holding her finger against her lips. "Shhh. Just listen."

The Queen continued. "For as long as anyone can remember, I've always left a little gift for each tooth to say 'Thank you' and — "

This time, it was Washington who interrupted. "Me giff?" He was trying to wobble his bottom tooth.

QQ smiled. "Of course ... once that tooth comes out." She continued, "This year, we decided to do something extra special for the children called — "

Tulip was about to interrupt when a pat on her shoulder signalled for her to pinch her lips together to stop herself from interrupting once again.

QQ went on, "It's called Shimmer-Shire Sunday. For the very first time, children will be invited to see where we fairies live. It will be our one-day-a-year Festival of Fairies. Children will be allowed to visit all five towers ..." She paused. "Uh, four towers, actually. For security reasons, we can't allow visitors in *this* tower, except under the strictest supervision."

Tulip's hand shot up. "Is it because of the Ding and the Globe?"

QQ nodded. "Right. I *knew* you were brainy. When I tell you my problem, I *know* you'll be brave, too."

Tulip's hand dropped down quickly. *Me and my big mouth*, she muttered to herself.

The Fairy Queen continued. "Children will love eating the tasty treats in the Fairy Feast, bouncing in the dragon castle, watching fairy dust being made, and even learning a magic trick or two from Merlin and Maxima."

"Sounds perfect," murmured Tulip, "just perfect."

QQ sighed a huge sigh. It was so huge, it fluttered her wings. It made the QQ-Ding ding and the QQ-Globe glow. "Yes, perfect except for one thing. The newest, most exciting fun of all, the very reason we decided to have Shimmer-Shire Sunday, will be missing."

"Missing? Why?" Tulip asked.

Queen Quinella cleared her throat. "Well, imagine this — the tallest, most shimmery amusement ever, and it's made entirely out of baby teeth. But, now, just two days before the first ever Shimmer-Shire Sunday, we've run out of teeth … baby *molar* teeth to be exact."

"Me give toof," Washington said, still trying to wiggle one of his front teeth.

That made QQ laugh … for a moment.

Tulip looked puzzled. "You mean, kids stopped putting their teeth under their pillows?"

"Oh, no, nothing like that. I've collected baby teeth as usual but, somehow, all my precious baby *molars* have been disappearing as fast as I collect them. Someone is stealing them from the tower where Catcher and Cricket, the tooth keepers, live. And that means we can't finish building the most amazing amusement for Shimmer-Shire Sunday." A little tear slid down the Fairy Queen's cheek.

Poppy put her arm around her big sister and nodded to Tulip. "Now, do you see why I came for you?"

Tulip frowned. "Uh, not really. First of all, I don't even know what the tallest, most shimmery amusement is and, second of all, I don't know why baby molars are missing. By the way, what *is* a baby molar?"

"Before I confuse you even more, let me teach you about your teeth." Queen Quinella waved her wand again and, in an instant, a set of teeth appeared on her lap. A set of plastic teeth. "This is what your baby teeth look like," she said, opening and closing the teeth. "Did you know you have 20 baby teeth in all?"

Tulip and Washington shook their heads. "Does that mean you come to my house 20 times?" Tulip asked.

"If you put each of your baby teeth under your pillow, you can be sure I'll come 20 times." She opened the plastic jaws. "See these four front teeth on the top and these four on the bottom?" She ran her fingers over the teeth.

Washington and Tulip nodded. At the same time, a little mirror magically appeared in each of their hands.

"Now, look at your own teeth in your mirrors."

They looked.

"See, you have the same eight teeth. They're called *incisors*." She paused. "Except you, Tulip. You have only seven, right? I hope the other one is waiting for me under your pillow."

"It is."

"Me eight sizus," Washington said, feeling his incisors and trying to wobble one of them.

QQ opened the jaws a little wider. "Now, these two pointy teeth on each side of the incisors are called *canines*. You have two on the top and two on the bottom."

Washington looked in his mirror and counted. "One, two, fwee, foah."

"Nice counting," said the Queen. "Now, look here again." She opened the jaws even wider. "In the very back of your mouth, you have four flat *molars* on the bottom and four more on the top. That's another eight baby teeth. So, if you add them all up, do you remember how many I said you have?"

Tulip's hand shot up. "Eight plus four plus eight equals … 20!"

"Exactly! I knew you were brainy! Now, as I said, our tallest, most shimmery amusement is made entirely out of molars. It's called The Molar Coaster."

"The Molar Coaster!" Tulip burst out laughing. "Is that a roller coaster made of molars?"

"Exactly," said Poppy. "And without molars, we can't put the finishing touches on our super special Molar Coaster for Shimmer-Shire Sunday."

Queen Quinella sighed. "We tried to keep it a secret, but I think someone stole our idea and most of our baby molars! We're in big trouble!"

Chapter 9

The Queen of the Tooth Fairies looked straight at Tulip. "Now do you understand why I sent Poppy to your house?"

Tulip nodded. "I understand, but it makes no sense. Who would steal baby molars? Nobody wants them besides *you*, the real, genuine Tooth Fairy. Who else collects baby teeth? Who else leaves a little thank-you gift? Nobody, that's who."

"Me yike giff," Washington said.

QQ ruffled Washington's hair. "And you'll get one after you lose that tooth you're wiggling. Promise." She turned back to Tulip. "It seems so greedy, so silly, and so downright mean for someone to steal our baby molars when all we want is to bring joy and happiness to children. I just can't imagine who would do such a thing."

Tulip shrugged her shoulders. "Beats me, but I think you're right about it being someone greedy, silly, and — suddenly,

Tulip interrupted herself. "Wait a minute! Did you say greedy, silly, and *mean*?"

QQ sighed. "Yes, it seems that way to me."

Tulip wrinkled her forehead like she was deep in thought and quietly said, "Hmmm." She looked like she was having a conversation with herself. "Hmmm," she said again. "I wonder … could it be … no, no way … and,

yet — "

QQ slid to the edge of her throne to get a closer look at Tulip. "What? What do you wonder? Do you have an idea?"

"Maybe. It seems really crazy, but maybe … maybe … it could be — "

"Who?" demanded QQ. "Who could it be? You must tell me right away!"

"Whoa!" Tulip raised both hands like she was stopping traffic. "I really have no idea except —"

"Except what?" This time, it was Poppy asking the questions. "Did you hear something? Or see something? Or feel something?"

Tulip took a deep breath. "Do you remember when we were flying to Shimmer-Shire, and we looked down — "

"Sure," Poppy interrupted. "That's when you asked me what a hillock is."

Tulip nodded. "Right."

"And I said it's what fairies call a small hill."

"Right," Tulip nodded again.

Poppy went on. "And then I pointed to a hillock that looks different from all the other hillocks. Most have flat tops, but that one has a round dome top with wonky-looking tree-thingies sticking out of it."

Tulip nodded for the third time. "Right, and when I saw the round-dome hillock, I wondered why it looked familiar."

"But that's not possible," Poppy said quickly. "You've never been here before."

Tulip said "Right" for the fourth time. Then she added, "I wanted to fly over to check it out, but you said we had to hurry to see QQ. So, I rushed after you, and then I got so excited about seeing Shimmer-Shire, I forgot all about the weird-looking hillock."

QQ looked back and forth and forth and back between Poppy and Tulip. "This conversation is twisting my brain into a fairy fuzz. There are hillocks everywhere around Shimmer-Shire. What could one funny-looking one possibly have to do with our missing molars?"

Tulip shrugged. "I don't know, but I do know one thing — there's only one way to find out."

"How?" asked Poppy.

"Pay that funny-looking hillock a visit."

Poppy sucked in her breath. "Oooh, I don't think that's a good idea. You never know who's friendly or not so friendly to us Shimmer-Shire fairies."

Tulip's eyes popped wide open. "No way!"

"Yes, way," Pansy said. "My sister is right. Sometimes other fairies or gremlins or goblins get jealous out here in Fairyland, so we have to be very careful."

Queen Quinella agreed. "But," she said, "we're in a pinch. Shimmer-Shire Sunday is just two days away. We can't waste any more time." She looked at Tulip. "Now that I see you're brave enough to check out that strange hillock, I have hope that Shimmer-Shire Sunday will still go on."

All of a sudden, after hearing Poppy's warning, Tulip didn't feel all that brave ... or that brainy. In fact, she wished she'd never even suggested checking out the hillock. Just because there was something about it that had caught her attention and given her tummy flutters, that didn't mean she should pay it a visit.

Queen Quinella went on, "We fairies have given up trying to solve our problem. Now, we're counting on *you*, Tulip. You're our only hope for saving Shimmer-Shire Sunday."

Chapter 10

Tulip gulped. "But, I —"

Queen Quinella leaned down and gently squeezed Tulip's shoulders. "I'll help you in every way I can. Just tell me what you need."

Tulip's first thought was this — *I need to get out of here.*

Her second thought was the same as her first — *I need to get out of here,* but when she looked around at QQ and Poppy and Pansy and saw how worried they were, she quickly had a third thought: *Okay, I'll check out the hillock. But after that, I'll fly straight home to Lilac Village. I'll be very sorry if there's no super-special Molar Coaster for Shimmer-Shire Sunday, and I'll be even more sorry to disappoint QQ and Poppy and Pansy, but —*

Tulip felt a tug on her PJs. "C'on, Tooyip. We be bwave. Go see heeyuck."

"Thank you," Queen Quinella said. "I knew I could count on you Twinkles." She turned to Tulip. "Please hurry. Time is running out."

The fairy queen slid a shiny golden ring on Tulip's finger. "There's enough fairy dust in this for you and Washington to fly back to Shimmer-Shire. Just sprinkle a tiny speck on your heads and, before you know it, you'll be flying."

Tulip hurried to the door of the royal chamber. She paused and looked back. Her little brother was still standing there; he hadn't moved. "C'mon, Washington. Don't be a slow-poke."

With a worried look, he hurried over to his sister. "Twuffle fry back, too?"

"Of course. We won't leave Truffle behind."

"No faiwee duss fo Twuffle," he said, holding back tears.

Queen Quinella saw Washington's sad face. At first, she didn't understand why he was almost crying. Then, she tapped herself lightly on the head. "Dear me, how could I forget Truffle! I'm so sorry. Come here, Truffle."

The basset hound padded over to the queen. She bent down and stroked his long, soft ears.

Truffle woofed and waggled his head from side to side. Every waggle made a rattle.

Queen Quinella heard it. "What's that rattle?"

Truffle woofed and waggled his head again.

QQ ran her fingers around Truffle's neck. That's when she discovered the little treat box hitched to his collar. She slid open the lid. Truffle's doggy treats were still inside, but there was plenty of room to fit in a golden, heart-shaped bag filled with fairy dust. "Here's enough dust for you and a bit extra ... just in case you need it."

Truffle wagged his tail. Tulip and Washington waited by the door. They couldn't see what the queen did or hear a word she said.

QQ and Truffle joined Tulip and Washington. With her magic wand, she tapped all three Twinkles' heads. "You're all set to go. Good luck!"

Tulip was about to remind QQ once again that she was only seven-going-on-eight, but before she could say 'seven-going' — Tulip found herself and her little brother and their basset hound outside the Queen's tower. Then, as if by magic, the three Twinkles were flying over the moat that surrounded the castle, and over the unicorns and little fairy cottages, and over the half-built, super-special Molar Coaster. They were heading straight for the strange-looking hillock in the distance.

Chapter 11

Tulip wished she felt braver. She wished she felt brainier. Most of all, she wished she were heading back to her own warm bed in Lilac Village, where her tooth was safely hidden under her pillow.

As the Twinkles flew closer to the dome-shaped hill, Tulip again felt flutters in her tummy. She asked herself, *Where have I seen those wonky-looking tree-thingies sticking out of a round top? Why do they look familiar? And why do they fill me with jitters?*

With Tulip in the lead and Washington and Truffle close behind, the three Twinkles flew slower and slower and lower and lower. Finally, their feet touched gently on the ground. They had landed so close to the hillock that Tulip could almost reach out and touch it.

And that's when her eyes popped wide open. And so did her mouth.

That's when she knew exactly what had given her tummy flutters.

That's when she knew those things sticking out of the round hillock weren't trees.

And they weren't TV antennae.

And they weren't star-tracking telescopes.

No.

They were letters.

And not just any letters.

They were **M**'s.

Four big **M**'s.

And she knew they didn't stand for **M**onday or **M**oana or **M**ickey **M**ouse.

"Oh, no!" groaned Tulip. "Not him again."

Chapter 12

There was no doubt about it. Tulip knew exactly what the letters stood for — **M**ugsy **M**aldoom's **M**arvelous **M**ogadome!

Just moments after Tulip recognized Mugsy's mogadome, Washington recognized it, too. "Mugsy dome!" he cried out.

"Right, Washington. That silly 'ol troll tried to disguise the letters with branches and leaves. He's such a troublemaker; I wonder what he's up to now."

Tulip had not forgotten how Mugsy had tried to ruin Santa's Christmas. She also clearly remembered how he had almost ruined the Easter Bunny's egg hunt.

"Mugsy twubble!" Washington yelled, shaking his finger at the mogadome. "Bad Mugsy!"

"Shhh," his sister whispered. "We don't want him to know we're here." She wagged her finger at Truffle. "No woofing, Truffle … and no sneezing." When the Twinkles had touched the ground, Truffle landed in a patch of yellow dandelions. And even though they always made him sneeze, Truffle *loved* dandelions.

Tulip hadn't noticed the dandelions at first. She was too worried about her discovery — the discovery about who might be behind the missing molars. "We'd better take a look around and … " She paused and patted Truffle's soft head … "and get you outta' this sneeze-patch, fast!"

The soft flutter of three pairs of fairy wings was the only sound that could be heard as the Twinkles rose up, up, up off the ground. Looking down, they saw the mogadome was surrounded by a dark, muddy moat — it smelled like dirty socks. An old, rickety, wooden bridge with missing boards led over the water to the front door of the dome. Broken chairs, tables, rusty machines, and one-wheeled bicycles lay stacked up in piles next to the mogadome. Gliding silently, Tulip led her brother and Truffle around to the back of the dome.

What she saw made her gulp.

Chapter 13

Here's why Tulip gulped:

On top of a gate made of rusty bed springs was a lopsided, wooden sign. In big, wobbly, cock-eyed letters it said,

MUGZEEZ MAGIK KINGDUMB

OPPENING SUNDAA

MOLER MOBEEL RIDZ: $2

"Mugsy could use some spelling lessons," Tulip muttered. "And that's not all. The sign makes no sense. Mugsy doesn't have a magic kingdom, and whoever heard of a moler mobeel!"

Tulip flew lower to get a better look behind the gate. She especially wanted to see what Mugsy's Moler Mobeel looked like. But it wasn't a moler mobeel she saw.

She saw Mugsy!

The troll was stepping out from behind something that looked like a mountain of junk.

And just when she saw *him*, he saw *her*.

"Well, well, look who's come for a visit," he called up to the Twinkles. "Is it Three-lips? Four-lips? I can't remember."

"TU. LIP!" Tulip snapped.

"Oh, yes. And I see you brought your cute little brother and that floppy-eared pooch. Whutta' you doin' here?"

"More to the point, whutta' *you* doin' here?"

"Wouldn't you like to know, Miss Daisy."

Tulip replied in her sweetest voice. "Oh, very much, Mr Mugsy."

"I'll give you a tour. C'mon down."

More than anything, Tulip did not want to 'c'mon down.' But she had come this far, and she'd agreed to help Queen Quinella.

She couldn't disappoint the Queen of the Fairies.

Or could she?

Tulip hovered over the troll, wondering what to do. Should she fly back to Shimmer-Shire? Should she fly back to Lilac Village? Should she forget all about the missing molars? What should she do?

Here's what she decided to do:

First, fly back to Shimmer-Shire, tell Queen Quinella she was very, very sorry, but she couldn't find the missing molars.

Second, fly back to Lilac Village and forget all about the fairies.

That's what she decided to do.

Chapter 14

But, that's *not* what she did.

"Okay," she called down, "but make it quick. I'm busy."

As soon as all three Twinkles touched down on the ground, the troll stepped up to Tulip. "Well, Miss Petunia, it's your lucky day."

Tulip didn't bother to correct Mugsy. She just rolled her eyes and looked the troll up and down. He was still wearing a red cowboy hat with fake bunny ears sticking out of the top. His nose looked even bigger and rounder than the last time she saw him. A rope around his fat tummy held up his baggy pants, and he wore cardboard sandals held on with rubber bands. "You look terrible," she said.

Mugsy parked his fists on his waist and stuck out his chest. "I think I look quite handsome. What do you suggest?"

"For starters, I suggest you get rid of the cowboy hat and bunny ears."

"Don't be rude," snapped the troll. "You haven't even admired my delicate fairy wings." He did a little twirl. Tied to Mugsy's back were brown, square, cardboard wings that almost flopped off when he twirled. "Me and all my mogsters have them. You do remember my brave little mogsters, don't you, Miss Sunflower?"

"How could I forget your poor little mini-Mugsys who do everything you tell them to do. I feel sorry for them." Tulip heaved a sigh. "So, what's up?"

"As I was saying, Miss Rosebud, it's your lucky day. Me and my mogsters are putting the finishing touches on my one-of-a-kind Moler Mobeel and my one-and-only Moler Mountain. They've gotta' be finished in two days for the opening of —"

"Of what?" Tulip snapped. *Shimmer-Shire Sunday is also just two days away,* she said to herself. *Hmmm, I wonder if —*

"Patience, please," Mugsy said in a sugary sweet voice. "Didn't you read the sign — Mugzeez Magick Kingdumb? I've invited kids from all over the world to take rides up my spectacular Moler Mountain in my spectacular Moler Mobeel."

"Sounds pretty spectacular. Can we see them?"

"Open your eyes." Mugsy waved his arm in a half-circle at the pile of junk he was standing next to. It was taller than the mogadome. "Ta Da! Moler Mountain!"

Tulip wrinkled her forehead. "Are you kidding me?" She moved closer to examine Mugsy's so-called mountain. "Looks more like a pile of icky teeth."

"Clever Violet," Mugsy chuckled. "Teeth it is."

"Whose teeth?"

"Cows and horses and pigs and rabbits and deer and — " He took a breath. "My mogsters find them in the tall grass all around here."

"So that's it! *You're* the one who's trying to copy Queen Quinella! *You're* the one who wants to ruin Shimmer-Shire Sunday!"

Chapter 15

Mugsy smiled and nodded. "Clever again, Miss Bluebell."

Tulip shook her head. "Your idea won't work. No one's going to fall for it. Queen Quinella collects shiny-white baby teeth, not broken, grubby teeth like this." She pulled a green-and-brown-stained tooth from the pile. "And she made a shimmering castle with towers and — "

Mugsy interrupted. "Castle schmashel. See those tracks running up my mountain? For just $2 each, kids will ride straight up and down *my* shimmering Moler Mountain in *my* shimmering Moler Mobeel. They'll love it more than anything at Shimmer-Shire."

"Doubt it," Tulip muttered. "Once Queen Quinella finishes

her Molar Coaster, children will love it way more than your silly straight-up-and-down —" Suddenly, Tulip cupped her hand over her mouth. "Oh, no! Forget what I just said about —"

Mugsy laughed a nasty, trollish laugh. "Too late. My adorable mogsters already told me about the Molar Coaster. That's how I got the idea for *my* Moler Mobeel. Follow me, Miss Lilypad. I have something to show you."

Silently, the three Twinkles followed Mugsy in his flip-flopping cardboard sandals. Tulip couldn't imagine what was on the other side of his mountain. One thing she knew for sure — it would be no match for Queen Quinella's Molar Coaster.

"Ta Da! — my one-of-a-kind Moler Mobeel!" Mugsy again waved his arm in a half-circle at something also made of icky, green-and-brown-stained, broken teeth.

Tulip squinted at Mugsy's creation. "Looks like a dirty ol' bathtub to me."

"Have you no imagination? Once it has its shimmery finish, it'll be the most marvelous Moler Mobeel ever!"

"Doubt it," Tulip muttered again. She walked slowly around the bathtub thingamajig. "It's got old, rusty wheels, and there's nothing marvelous about it."

The troll rubbed his hands together and laughed a laugh that sent prickles up and down Tulip's spine. "Hee, hee, hee, Miss Marigold. Get ready for the biggest marvel of all!"

Chapter 16

Without another word, Mugsy slip-slopped on his cardboard sandals to a wide-open door. The door led straight into the mogadome. "C'mon," he yelled.

Tulip didn't c'mon.

Neither did Washington. "Me no yike dome," he said.

Tulip glanced down at her little brother. He had stuck his thumb in his mouth and his finger in his nose. That's what he did when he got nervous. And scared. Why was he nervous and scared? He remembered when Mugsy had trapped the Twinkles in the mogadome. The first time he caught them in a net, and another time he locked them in an egg-making machine.

Tulip squeezed Washington's hand. "I know what you're thinking, and I'm nervous, too. But, Queen Quinella is depending on us. Hold onto Truffle's collar with your other hand. We won't let Mugsy trap us this time."

Washington did what his sister told him to do and, slowly, very slowly, the Twinkles shuffled to the door of the mogadome.

"Ta Da!" Mugsy bellowed proudly. "My glistening beauties!"

At first, Tulip couldn't make out what she was looking at. As her eyes got used to the darkness inside the dome — trolls don't like sunshine — she began to figure it out. Here's what Tulip saw:

1. On the ground, a huge circle of shiny-white baby molars.

2. Dozens of mogsters with toothbrushes.

3. Dozens of mogsters polishing thousands of baby molars with their toothbrushes.

Mugsy chuckled. "Wanna' hear my clever plan?" He didn't wait for Tulip's answer. "My mogsters will bubblegum these shiny-white baby molers onto my Moler Mobeel and my Moler Mountain. They'll be even more spectacular than the Fairy Queen's Moler Koaster."

Tulip sighed, "I should have guessed you'd do something like this."

Just then, Washington dropped Tulip's hand and Truffle's collar and dashed over to the teeth. He grabbed a handful and let them sift through his fingers. He raced back to Tulip. "We fine QQ teef!"

"Yup, these are her missing molars, alright. No doubt about it." She turned to Mugsy. "Did you really think you'd get away with stealing QQ's precious teeth?"

Mugsy shrugged. "It's just her molers. No big deal."

"It *is* a big deal! You want to spoil Shimmer-Shire Sunday! Shame on you."

Mugsy puffed out his chest. "MUGZEEZ MAGIK KINGDUMB is going to be way more fun than her … her … skimmer … spire … funday."

Tulip rolled her eyes. "It's *Shimmer. Shire. Sunday*. And it's going to be The. Best. Sunday. Ever."

"Don't. Be. So. Sure, Miss Thistle."

"Oh, I'm sure."

"If you're so sure, how about taking a ride in my marvelous Moler Mobeel … for free! And your cute little brother and that floppy-eared pooch can go, too … for free!"

The last thing Tulip wanted was a ride in Mugsy's Moler Mobeel.

The *first* thing she wanted was to get QQ's precious molars back to Shimmer-Shire … ASAP!

But how?

She *had* to figure that out … fast!

Chapter 17

Tulip did *not* want a ride in the Moler Mobeel *but*, she thought, *I'll do it anyway. It'll give me time to think. Time to figure out how to get QQ's molars back to Shimmer-Shire.* "Okay, we'd *love* a ride."

The troll grinned a big, toothy grin. "You won't be sorry." He cleared his throat and yelled, "Mogsters, drop your toothbrushes. Haul the Moler Mobeel over to Moler Mountain and put it on the track. Our lovely surprise guests can't wait for a ride!"

The mogsters swarmed out of the mogadome and over to the Moler Mobeel. After much shifting and shoving and grunting and groaning, they pushed the green-and-brown-stained, toothy mobeel onto the track that led up Moler Mountain.

Tulip helped her little brother and Truffle climb into the mobeel. "Me no yike," Washington mumbled.

"Me no yike either," Tulip whispered, climbing in after him.

"Ready. Set. Go!" Mugsy pulled a lever attached to the bottom of the track.

Nothing happened.

He pulled again.

Still nothing.

"Me yout!" Washington cried, lifting one leg over the side.

Mugsy pulled harder on the lever. This time, the mobeel bumped and jerked and thumped and humped as it slowly took off, struggling to climb up the track. By the time it had nearly reached the top, the screeching and rattling and hissing had grown so loud that Tulip and Washington had to cover their ears. Even Truffle hid his ears under his paws.

"How's the ride?" Mugsy shouted from below. "Beauty, huh?"

Tulip held up two thumbs. "The buh-buh-best," she yelled, bouncing up and down.

At the top of the mountain, the mobeel chugged to a stop.

"Fantastic view!" Tulip called down. "I can even see Shimmer-Shire!"

"I told you it would be marvelous." The troll grinned a big, self-satisfied grin and shook his fist in the direction of Shimmer-Shire. "Tough noodles, Queen Vanilla. Mugzeez Magick Kingdumb is numero uno."

"It's number one for sure," Tulip agreed. "Kids won't want to go to boring ol' Shimmer-Shire when they can come here instead. Now, how about bringing us down so your mogsters can get busy bubblegumming all those shiny, white baby molars."

"I knew you'd see it my way." The troll pulled the lever. The Moler Mobeel chugged and rattled and screeched its way down the pile of teeth.

At the bottom, Tulip climbed out first, then helped Washington. Truffle hopped out by himself. "That was truly awesome! You *must* see the view … right now!" (What Tulip didn't say was that getting Mugsy into the mobeel would give her more time to come up with a plan. A plan to save Shimmer-Shire Sunday.)

"But my mogsters have fabillions and katrillions of molers to stick on before my — "

"Don't worry, there's plenty of time. It's way more important for you to ride to the top, immediately! Your kingdom looks truly magical from up there."

Mugsy snorted. "Told ya so, but … let me think." He scratched his tummy. He scratched his chin. He scratched his nose. "Hmmm … well … maybe you're right, Miss Marshmallow. Bubblegumming can wait. Here I go!"

With a helping push from Tulip and several mogsters, Mugsy climbed into the Moler Mobeel. He gave two thumbs up.

"Pull the lever, Miss Snapdragon, and let 'er rip!"

Tulip pulled the lever. After a great deal of squeaking and hissing, the Moler Mobeel started jerking up the mountain. When he reached the top, Mugsy waved, grinning from ear to ear. "Hey, mogsters, look at me!"

The mogsters waved back. Then they all joined hands and, like a swarm of honey bees, returned to their job in the mogadome.

Tulip gave Mugsy a thumbs-up. "Take your time. Relax. Enjoy your marvelous view." She turned to Washington and whispered, "I'm getting worried. I haven't thought of an idea yet. Time is running out ... fast!"

Chapter 18

"I can't waste any more time here," Tulip muttered. She let go of the lever. "C'mon, Truffle. You, too, Washington." She headed straight back to the mogadome.

Washington didn't move. "Me no yike mogdome," he said. "Me here."

"No, Washington. We Twinkles have to stick together. We're Queen Quinella's only hope."

Muttering under his breath and dragging his feet with every step, Washington trudged over to his sister.

Truffle bounded after Washington, but he didn't stop beside him. He headed straight into the mogadome. Tulip and Washington followed.

Inside, the mogsters were busy polishing the baby molars. They paid no attention to the three Twinkles. They also paid no attention to the loud shouting now coming from the top of Moler Mountain.

Tulip *did* pay attention. She stepped back outside the mogadome. From the mobeel, Mugsy was waving his fists like crazy. "Hey! Can't you hear anything? I've seen the view. Get me down … NOW!"

"Oh dear, how could I have forgotten you?" Tulip called in her sweetest voice. She hurried over to Moler Mountain, grabbed the lever, and pulled. (Actually, Tulip didn't really pull; she just pretended to pull.)

The mobeel didn't move.

"Don't worry, I'll have you down in a sec."

She pretended to pull again.

Nothing happened.

"Wait right there, Mugsy. I'll get the mogsters to help."

"I'm getting impatient," he yelled. "Very, very impatient."

"I'm so sorry to keep you waiting. Your lovely mogsters will be here ASAP!"

Tulip walked slowly, slowly back to the mogadome thinking, *I*

can't keep Mugsy in the mobeel much longer. He's getting madder by

the minute.

Inside the mogadome, Washington was watching the busy, toothbrushing mogsters. But where was Truffle? Tulip looked all around the dark, gloomy dome for the basset hound. He was nowhere to be seen. *Oh no! Has Truffle taken off? Has he gone back to Shimmer-Shire? Or, worse, to Lilac Village?*

Tulip rubbed her eyes to get a clearer look. She searched the dome again. This time, she spotted him. The basset hound was way over on the other side of the circle of molars. His nose was near the ground. He was sniffing.

"Come, Truffle," Tulip called.

Truffle didn't come.

She called louder. "Truffle, COME!"

Truffle stayed put.

"Okay then, I'm coming to get you," Tulip snapped. "We have to stay together." She started walking around the circle of molars. Before she was even halfway to the basset hound, she saw what he was sniffing — a clump of wilted, yellow flowers.

Dandelions! His favorite!

"Get outta' the dandelions, Truffle," Tulip called. "They make you sneeze."

Just as she said *sneeze*, the basset hound sneezed. Not one, not two, but three sneezes. With each sneeze, the lid on his treat box slid a little more open. Then came sneeze number four and, with it, off fell the lid. All his precious doggie treats dropped to the ground. Truffle bent down to gobble them up but, instead of gobbling, he sneezed.

And sneezed.

One more gigantic sneeze and a little, golden, heart-shaped bag fell to the ground and burst wide open. It was the bag Queen Quinella had secretly slipped into Truffle's treat box. The bag was filled with magic fairy dust — the very same dust Queen Quinella had put in the ring she gave to Tulip.

What happened next made Tulip gasp!

Chapter 19

After the bag burst open, Truffle sneezed six more non-stop sneezes. With every sneeze, fairy dust spread out wider and wider above the shiny white teeth. Soon, the cloud of dust hovered in the air, directly over the circle of baby teeth.

With their mouths hanging open, the three Twinkles stared at the cloud. What would happen next?

Here's what happened:

Tiny bits of glittery dust drifted down, down, down. The moment a speck of dust landed on a molar, something magic happened. It was more magical than Tulip could ever imagine. Each grain of dust suddenly burst into a tiny, delicate set of fairy wings. The fluttering wings came in all colors of the rainbow. "They look like dancing butterflies," Tulip murmured.

"Toof now fry?" Washington asked.

"Maybe," his big sister answered. "I wonder if ..." She paused, and as she watched the gently fluttering wings, she had a thought — *It's worth a try.* She cleared her throat and stepped closer to the circle of molars. "Fly to Shimmer-Shire," she said loud enough to be heard on the other side of the mogadome.

Nothing happened.

"Fly to Shimmer-Shire and Queen Quinella," she said in an even louder voice.

Again, nothing happened.

Washington took Tulip's hand. "Toof not fry?"

"Not yet. I'll try one more time." Tulip cleared her throat and shouted, "Fly to Shimmer-Shire and Queen Quinella and the Molar Coaster!"

At first, it looked like nothing was going to happen.

Then, the delicate wings began fluttering faster. And a little faster. And faster still until, before the Twinkles' amazed eyes, the beautiful, shiny baby molars rose up and up and up and straight out the door of the mogadome.

Chapter 20

Tulip, Washington, and Truffle dashed outside. So did the mogsters. They watched in wonder as thousands of baby molars soared past Mugsy, trapped in his Moler Mobeel on top of Moler Mountain.

Mugsy also watched in wonder. "Whoa! What's going on? What am I looking at?" He rubbed his eyes. "What *are* those things? Flying marbles? Eggs? Puff balls?" He banged his fists harder and harder on the Moler Mobile. "Get me down, right now!"

Tulip didn't move. Neither did Washington or Truffle. Neither did the mogsters. They all watched as the molars flew over the mogadome and the stinky moat and the sign that said

MUGZEEZ MAGIK KINGDUMB

OPPENING SONDAA

MOLER MOBEEL RIDZ: $2

They watched until the teeth disappeared from sight, heading straight for Shimmer-Shire and Queen Quinella's castle.

Washington jumped up and down yelling, "Toof fry! Toof fry!"

His excitement was cut short by a very angry shout from atop Moler Mountain. "Hey, down there! Has everybody forgotten about me?" Mugsy stomped his feet. "Mogsters, hurry up and get me outta' here! You've got a whole lotta work to do before — "

"So sorry, Mugsy," Tulip called up. "I forgot to tell them you wanted to come down, but there's really no need to hurry because — "

"Toof gone!" Washington yelled. "Toof fry!"

"What's that little brat talking about?" Mugsy bellowed.

Tulip smiled. "You'll see when you get down here. It's a magic surprise. Now, if you'll excuse me, I've got some magic of my own to do."

Without another word, she slipped off the ring Queen Quinella had given her. She opened the tiny cap on the top and tapped first Truffle's head, then Washington's, then her own. *Please let this work*, she begged to herself. *Take us to Shimmer-Shire … please.*

In an instant, the ring vanished, and the pink, butterfly-shaped wings on their backs began to flutter. In another instant, the three Twinkles floated slowly up, up, and up. They drifted up over the mogadome, up over the stinky moat, and up past Mugsy. He was still waving his fists and yelling something about fairies and molers and Queen Vanilla.

"It's Queen Quinella," Tulip yelled back. "Get it straight, Bugsy. Bye, bye."

Chapter 21

"I see it! I see the castle!" Tulip called.

"Me see, too," echoed Washington.

Truffle woofed.

"And the lights are on in Queen Quinella's tower. Think she's waiting for us?"

Before her little brother could answer, Tulip felt her wings flutter slower and slower until the tip of her toes lightly touched the ground. Washington and Truffle touched down beside her. She was about to knock softly on the golden door of the tower when, to her surprise, the door swung open.

It was Poppy. "We've been waiting for you. After all the molars flew back, we knew you'd be close behind. C'mon in. QQ is so excited to see you."

The Twinkles followed Poppy to the queen's chamber. She was sitting on her royal throne with Pansy standing next to her. Before Tulip could say 'Hello,' all three fairies were hugging the Twinkles, exclaiming, "Thank you, thank you, thank you. You did it!"

Washington wriggled out of the group hug. "Toof fry, toof fry!" he cried, his eyes wide open with wonder.

Queen Quinella smiled and ruffled Washington's hair. "Yes, they did, and my fairies have already put the final molars on the Molar Coaster. Would you Twinkles like to be the first to have a ride and then — ?"

"YES! YES!" Tulip and Washington shouted before the queen could finish her sentence. Truffle woofed and wagged.

Queen Quinella held up both hands like she was stopping traffic. "And, then, before you go home, I thought you might like to stop at Fairy Feast for a little snack and, after that, drop into Awesome Amusements for some bouncing in the dragon bouncy castle. Sound good?"

"YES! YES!"

"And, don't worry, I haven't forgotten Truffle."

At the sound of his name, the basset hound looked up at Queen Quinella. She tapped his collar with her wand. Instantly, a brand new treat-box filled with his favorite bone-shaped doggie treats hung from his collar. He licked both of the queen's bare feet. She chuckled. "Now, off with you, Twinkles. Enjoy Shimmer-Shire Sunday ... on Saturday!"

Chapter 22

"Time for breakfast, kids," Mrs Twinkle said softly the next morning. She stood beside Tulip's bed. "Did the tooth fairy come?"

Tulip rolled over, yawned, and rubbed her eyes. "You mean Queen Quinella?"

Her mother looked surprised. "I don't know the Tooth Fairy's name. I just wondered if she found your letter and your tooth."

Tulip felt under her pillow. The envelope was still there, but her letter and her tooth were gone.

"Did she leave you a little gift?"

Tulip tipped the envelope upside down. Out fell a ring. It looked very much like the ring filled with fairy dust that QQ had given her. She slipped it onto her finger. "Fits perfectly!"

"Must be magic," Mrs Twinkle said, smiling. "Now, come for breakfast, you two. Pancakes are getting cold."

Tulip and Washington, followed by Truffle, shuffled sleepily into the kitchen. They sat down at the table where a stack of warm pancakes was waiting. Tulip wiggled the tooth next to the gap in her mouth. "Wonder when I'll lose another one."

"Me yuse toof," Washington said.

Mr. Twinkle poured maple syrup on his pancakes. "You will soon, Kiddo."

"Me yuse toof," Washington said again, this time a little louder.

Mrs Twinkle served Tulip and Washington pancakes. "Don't worry, it'll come out when it's ready."

"Toof weddy NOW!" This time, Washington caught everyone's attention.

Mr and Mrs Twinkle and Tulip Twinkle put down their forks. They looked at

Washington. In his hand, he held a perfect, shiny, pure-white baby tooth.

The End

Note: **National Tooth Fairy Day** is celebrated twice a year — February 28 and August 22. Both dates are a great reminders for kids to take care of their precious teeth!

We hope that you enjoyed this title and look forward to many more to come. Please, leave us a review! Reviews matter to all of our authors.

Take a look at some of our other award-winning series at https://threeravenspublishing.com/series-universes/

Visit us at https://www.threeravenspublishing.com and sign up for our newsletter for the latest and greatest news on upcoming titles and events.

Other series and titles you might enjoy.

You can also keep up to date with our latest release announcements on Scifi.radio and get some of the best fandom programing on the planet.

Scifi for your Wifi

And don't forget to check out the latest edition of *Car Wars*

http://www.sjgames.com/car-wars/

Or the other amazing titles from
Steve Jackson Games

STEVE JACKSON GAMES

http://www.sjgames.com

…or the latest in the Car Warriors: Autoduel Chronicle fiction series.
https://threeravenspublishing.com/car-warriors-autoduel-chronicles/

www.ingramcontent.com/pod-product-compliance
Lightning Source LLC
Chambersburg PA
CBHW021652120626
46545CB00002B/831

* 9 7 8 1 9 6 6 5 0 7 4 0 6 *